DIGITIZE BUSINESS

AMAZING TIPS ON ONLINE DIGITIZATION

Charles Naylor P.

All right reserved. No part of this publication may be reproduced, distributed, or transmitted in any form or by any means, including photocopying, recording, or other electronic or mechanical method s, without the prior written permission of the publisher, except in the case of brief quotation embodied in critical reviews and certain other reviews and certain other noncommercial uses permitted by copyright law.

Copyright © Charles Naylor P., 2022

Table of content

Chapter 1: Computerized advertising:

Chapter 2: Figuring out Advanced Promoting

Chapter 3: Content Showcasing

Chapter 4: Partner promoting:

Chapter 5: Facebook Pages:

Chapter 6: Internet mentoring:

Chapter 7: Bring in Cash from Writing for a blog:

Chapter 1: Computerized advertising:

One more method for bringing in cash online without putting resources into versatile is through computerized promoting, which incorporates Website optimization, web-based entertainment, email showcasing, publishing content to a blog, and so on.

The term computerized showcasing alludes to the utilization of advanced channels to advertise items and administrations to arrive at customers. This kind of showcasing includes the utilization of sites, cell phones, web-based entertainment, web indexes, and other comparative channels.

Computerized promoting became famous with the appearance of the web during the 1990s.

Computerized promoting includes a portion of similar standards as customary showcasing and is many times considered another way for organizations to move toward purchasers and figure out their way of behaving. Organizations frequently consolidate conventional and computerized promoting methods in their systems.

Chapter 2: Figuring out Advanced Promoting

Showcasing alludes to any exercises that an organization uses to advance its items and administrations and further develop its portion of the overall industry. To find success, showcasing requires a blend of publicizing keen, deals, and the capacity to convey products to end-clients. This is typically embraced by unambiguous experts or advertisers who can work inside (for organizations) or remotely with other showcasing firms.

Customarily, organizations zeroed in on promoting through print, TV, and radio. Albeit these choices actually exist today, the ascent of the web prompted a change in the manner organizations arrived at buyers. That is where advanced advertising became possibly the most important factor. This type of showcasing includes the utilization of sites, online entertainment, web crawlers, applications — whatever integrates promoting with client input or a two-way collaboration between the organization and client.

Expanded innovation and more current patterns constrained organizations to meaningfully have an impact on the manner in which they advertised themselves. Email was a well known promoting device in the beginning of computerized showcasing. That center moved to web search tools like Netscape, which permitted organizations to tag and watchword stuff to get themselves taken note. The improvement of sharing locales like Facebook made it feasible for organizations to follow information to take care of customer patterns.

Cell phones and other computerized gadgets are currently making it more straightforward for organizations to showcase themselves alongside their items and administrations to purchasers. Concentrates on show that individuals favor utilizing their telephones to sign on to the web. So it ought to shock no one that 70% of people go with purchasing choices (typically on their telephones) before they really hit the buy button.1

Computerized advertising can be intelligent and is in many cases used to target explicit portions of the client base.

Exceptional Contemplations

Sponsors are regularly alluded to as sources, while individuals from the designated advertisements are generally called beneficiaries. Sources every now and again target profoundly unambiguous, distinct beneficiaries. For instance, in the wake of broadening the late-night hours, McDonald's designated shift laborers and explorers with computerized promotions on the grounds that the organization realized these individuals made up an enormous section of its late-night business. The organization urged them to download the Eatery Locater application, focusing on them with promotions put at robotized teller machines (ATMs), corner stores, and sites that its clients regularly visited.

Kinds of Computerized Showcasing Channels

As indicated above, showcasing was customarily finished through print (papers and magazines) and broadcast advertisements (television and radio). These are channels that actually exist today. Advanced promoting channels have developed and keep on doing as such. Coming up next are eight of the most well-known roads that organizations can take to support their promoting endeavors. Remember that a few organizations might involve various diverts in their endeavors.

Site Promoting

A site is the highlight of all computerized promoting exercises. It is an exceptionally strong channel all alone, but on the other hand it's the medium expected to execute an assortment of web based showcasing efforts. A site ought to address a brand, item, and administration in a reasonable and essential way. It ought to be quick, dynamic, and simple to utilize.

Pay-Per-Snap (PPC) Publicizing

Pay-per-click (PPC) promoting empowers advertisers to arrive at Web clients on various advanced stages through paid promotions. Advertisers can set up PPC crusades on Google, Bing, LinkedIn, Twitter, Pinterest, or Facebook and show their promotions to individuals looking for terms connected with the items or administrations.

PPC missions can section clients in light of their segment qualities, (for example, by age or orientation), or even objective their specific advantages or area. The most famous PPC stages are Google Promotions and Facebook Advertisements.

Chapter 3: Content Showcasing

The objective of content promoting is to arrive at possible clients using content. Content is typically distributed on a site and afterward advanced through virtual entertainment, email promoting, website streamlining, or even PPC crusades. The instruments of content showcasing incorporate web journals, digital books, online courses, infographics, web recordings, and online courses.

Email Promoting

Email promoting is as yet one of the best computerized showcasing channels. Many individuals mistake email promoting for spam email messages, however that is not the very thing email advertising is about. This kind of showcasing permits organizations to reach out to possible clients and anyone with any interest at all in their brands.

Numerous advanced advertisers utilize any remaining computerized showcasing channels to add prompts their email records and afterward, through email promoting, they make client obtaining pipes to transform those leads into clients.

Virtual Entertainment Promoting

The essential objective of a virtual entertainment promoting effort is brand mindfulness and laying out friendly trust. As you go further into web-based entertainment showcasing, you can utilize it to get leads or even as an immediate deals channel. Advanced posts and tweets are two instances of virtual entertainment promoting.

Partner Promoting

Subsidiary promoting is one of the most established types of advertising, and the web has carried new life to this old backup. With partner showcasing, powerhouses advance others' items and get a commission each time a deal is made or a lead is presented. Some notable organizations like Amazon have member programs that compensation out large number of dollars each month to sites that sell their items.

Video Showcasing

YouTube is one of the most famous web search tools on the planet. A ton of clients are going to YouTube prior to pursuing a purchasing choice, to learn something, read a survey, or just to unwind.

There are a few video promoting stages, including Facebook Recordings, Instagram, and even TikTok to use to run a video showcasing effort. Organizations make the most progress with video by coordinating it with Website design enhancement, content promoting, and more extensive web-based entertainment showcasing efforts.

SMS Informing

Organizations and not-for-profit associations additionally use SMS or instant messages to send data about their most recent advancements or give chances to willing clients. Political up-and-comers campaigning for office likewise use SMS message missions to spread positive data about their own foundation. As innovation has progressed, numerous message to-give crusades likewise permit clients to straightforwardly pay or give by means of a basic instant message.

Chapter 4: Partner promoting:

One of the most famous techniques for bringing in cash online without venture is associate showcasing.

This includes advancing items on your site and connecting them to an outer site or blog that will then impart a level of the deal to you when somebody purchases the item.

Member showcasing is a promoting model in which an organization repays outsider distributers to create traffic or prompts the organization's items and administrations. The outsider distributers are subsidiaries, and the commission charge boosts them to track down ways of advancing the organization.

Understanding Member Advertising

The web has expanded the conspicuousness of subsidiary showcasing. Amazon (AMZN) promoted the training by making an offshoot showcasing program by which sites and bloggers put connects to the Amazon page for a surveyed or examined item to get publicizing expenses when a buy is made. In this sense, partner showcasing is basically a compensation for-execution promoting program where the demonstration of selling is reevaluated across a tremendous organization.

Partner promoting originates before the Web, however in the realm of computerized showcasing, examination, and treats earned anything industry. An organization running a partner showcasing system can follow the connections that get leads and, through inside investigation, perceive the number of convert to deals.

An online business shipper needing to arrive at a more extensive base of web clients and customers might recruit a subsidiary. A member could be the proprietor of various sites or email advertising records; the more sites or email records that a partner has, the more extensive its organization. The recruited associate then imparts and advances the items presented on the web based business stage to their organization. The member does this by running standard promotions, message advertisements, posting joins on its sites, or sending messages to customers. Firms use commercials as articles, recordings, and pictures to cause a crowd of people to notice a help or item.

Guests who click the promotions or connections are diverted to the internet business webpage. Assuming that they buy the item or administration, the internet business dealer acknowledges the subsidiary's record for the settled upon commission, which could be 5% to 10% of the deals cost.

Extraordinary Contemplations

The objective of this model is to increment deals and make a mutually beneficial answer for both dealer and subsidiary. The framework is novel and beneficial and turning out to be progressively famous.

The web and further developing advances are making the model more straightforward to execute. Organizations have further developed how they track and pay commissions on qualified leads. Being better ready to follow leads and deals adds to how they can advance or better position their items.

Those keen on seeking after partner advertising will profit from figuring out what's required, as well as its benefits and drawbacks. Organizations looking for associates will profit from appropriately reviewing and qualifying their accomplices. In general, it is a minimal expense, powerful approach to promoting items and administrations, expanding brand mindfulness, and growing a shopper base.

Sorts of Subsidiary Advertising

There are three fundamental kinds of partner advertising: unattached subsidiary showcasing, related member promoting, and involved associate showcasing.

1. Unattached Partner Showcasing: This is a publicizing model in which the subsidiary has no association with the item or administration they are advancing. They have no known related abilities or skill and don't act as an expert on or make claims about its utilization. This is the most uninvolved type of subsidiary advertising. The absence of connection to the expected client and item vindicates the partner from the obligation to suggest or exhort.

2. Related Subsidiary Showcasing: As the name recommends, related partner advertising includes the advancement of items or administrations by a member with a relationship to the contribution of some sort. For the most part, the association is between the subsidiary's specialty and the item or administration. The subsidiary has sufficient impact and mastery to create traffic, and their degree of power makes them a confided in source. The partner, be that as it may, makes no cases about the utilization of the item or administration.

3. Involved Member Showcasing: This sort of showcasing lays out a more profound association between the partner and the item or administration they're advancing. They have utilized or right now utilize the item and are certain that their positive encounters can be shared by others. Their encounters are the notices, and they act as confided in wellsprings of data. Then again, on the grounds that they're giving suggestions, their standing might be undermined by any issues emerging from the contribution.

Benefits and Drawbacks of Associate Promoting

Partner showcasing can yield extraordinary awards for the publicizing organization and the subsidiary advertiser. The organization benefits from minimal expense promoting and the innovative showcasing endeavors of its members, and the associate advantages by acquiring extra pay and motivating forces. The profit from venture for partner advertising is high as the organization just pays on traffic changed over completely to deals. The expense of promoting, if any, is borne by the subsidiary.

The promoting organization sets the details of a member showcasing program. From the get-go, organizations to a great extent paid the expense per click (traffic) or cost per mile (impacts) on flag notices. As innovation advanced, the spotlight went to commissions on real deals or qualified leads. The early subsidiary promoting programs were defenseless against extortion since snaps could be created by programming, as could impressions.

Presently, most partner programs have severe agreements on the best way to create leads. There are likewise sure prohibited techniques, for example, introducing adware or spyware that divert all quest inquiries for an item to an offshoot's page. Some subsidiary showcasing programs venture to spread out how an item or administration is to be examined in the substance before a partner connection can be approved.

So a viable offshoot promoting program requires some thinking ahead. The agreements should be plainly illuminated, particularly in the event that the agreement understanding pays for traffic as opposed to deals. The potential for misrepresentation in member promoting is conceivable.

Corrupt members can hunch down space names with incorrect spellings and get a commission for the divert. They can populate online enlistment structures with counterfeit or taken data, and they can buy AdWords based on search conditions the organization as of now positions high on, etc. Regardless of whether the agreements are clear, a member showcasing program expects that somebody screen subsidiaries and implement rules. In return, notwithstanding, an organization can get to spurred, imaginative individuals, to assist with offering their items or administrations to the world.

Chapter 5: Facebook Pages:

They are a ton of ways of bringing in cash by Facebook. You can become Facebook page designer and connection it with your site or site page, then you will get compensated. Then again, assuming you have expertise recorded as a hard copy expositions and articles which suit to Facebook clients' advantage then you can likewise do this.

There are a lot more ways when it comes for bringing in cash through Facebook like schoolmates promoting on Facebook promotions and so on yet these tips I referenced above is sufficient from my side too on the grounds that today.

A Facebook page is a public profile made by organizations, associations, famous people and anybody looking to advance themselves freely through web-based entertainment. Facebook pages work similar as private profile pages, then again, actually they have "fans" rather than "companions." These pages are openly noticeable on the web and frequently post announcements, joins, occasions, photographs and recordings to their fans' news sources and walls.

Facebook pages give a way to organizations and different associations to collaborate with - as opposed to simply promote to - possible clients. They likewise give a basic center point of data about the page's proprietor.

Facebook pages outgrew Facebook gatherings, which were progressively being utilized by organizations and associations, but on the other hand were jumbled by a great deal of general vested parties. Not at all like page, Facebook bunches don't uphold Facebook Markup Language or Facebook applications, so pages gives significantly more usefulness.

A Facebook page might consolidate the accompanying:

- Organization/association outline

- Contact data

- Public statements

- RSS channels

- Twitter refreshes

- Organization news and announcements

- Client remarks/collaboration

Facebook pages can likewise be profoundly redone to show corporate logos and limited time items. Contingent upon the business, a Facebook page might be utilized to caution fans about forthcoming advancements or arrangements, or inquiry buyers about their inclinations. Applications can likewise be added to build a Facebook page's usefulness, permitting it to interface with a RSS channel or pertinent YouTube recordings. These capabilities permit a Facebook page to go about as a coordinated showcasing stage.

Online Work:

Online occupation is one of the internet based work without speculation which gives an ideal chance to bringing in cash on the web. With these positions, you really want not to take any sort of actual presence in office and can telecommute or concentrate too.

This occupation likewise offers better possibilities since it permits individuals to work from anyplace through PC or PC as it were.

Instagram page:

Instagram is a free web-based photograph sharing application and person to person communication stage that Facebook gained in 2012 however was recently sent off in 2010. Instagram permits clients to alter and transfer photographs and brief recordings through a portable application. Clients can add a title to every one of their posts and use area based hashtags and geotags to list these posts and have them looked for by different clients inside the application. Each post by a client shows up in their devotees' Instagram takes care of and can likewise be seen by the public while labeled utilizing hashtags or geotags. Clients additionally have the choice to make their profile private so just their adherents can see their posts.

Instagram for Business

Like such countless other interpersonal organizations, Instagram has turned into an incredible wellspring of productivity for organizations, a spot to cooperate with their clients and distribute their items. Instagram permits you to make business profiles with highlights one of a kind to this sort of record like examination measurements or publicizing items. The plan of Instagram is likewise wonderful as a grandstand since the plan has all the earmarks of being a sort of internet shopping. Furthermore, organization profiles are not by any means the only way that organizations need to publicize on Instagram, through powerhouses, client profiles with an enormous number of devotees, they can agree to advance their items. Among the benefits of involving Instagram for organizations are:

- Expanded perceivability.

- Improvement of the brand picture.

- Truly productive with regards to publicizing contrasted with different sites.

- Divert traffic to your site.

It associates with individuals who are keen on what you do or what's going on around them, it energizes their advantage towards things that they currently like and gives them more data about different things also, helping their taste improvement starting with one level then onto the next.

Chapter 6: Internet mentoring:

Internet mentoring is a business that can be extremely worthwhile. This implies it's not excessively difficult to bring in cash on the web (and something other than cash) from this sort of work.

The coaching ought to constantly be finished under the condition you keep up with 100 percent classification and respectability as an instructor, which guarantees your clients fill in certainty and construct entrust with their guides/educators - giving them better learning results after some time.

Web based mentoring is a virtual learning technique where poor tutees get help neighborhood, public along with global guides. Video conferencing notes sharing, email and a few different mediums are chiefly used to interface tutees with the mentors. They barely meet each other face to face.

How Online Mentors are Chosen?

Coaches are enlisted in various stages. They incorporate their capabilities, class and subjects they will educate, favored time, rate, and other significant subtleties on their profiles. A coach can show numerous subjects or one single subject - it is totally up to the mentors. Additionally, it is feasible to put the rate later.

Understudies or their folks also need to make a record to enroll their names on that stage. Then, tutees need to look for the subject/s they need educational cost. It is conceivable that an understudy is powerless in 1 or 2 explicit subjects - thus, they need to look for it.

Tutees will choose the mentor in light of their necessities, rating of the guide, charges for a subject and different elements.

Web based Mentoring Types

It should be evident that internet based mentors work on their own timetable and the quantity of tutees has no limits. Experienced web-based guides frequently give bunch educational cost utilizing various devices. Thus, that guide procures a colossal sum as educational expenses. Then again, guides offering individual educational cost need to make various openings for every understudy.

On the off chance that you are a novice, you might begin with individual educational cost. When you get a decent evaluating and survey, you can begin bunch educational cost.

How to Begin As A Web-based Mentor?

The most straightforward method for beginning as a web-based guide is to enlist on any stage that permits the mentor to enroll. These stages resemble an extension between the mentors and tutees. When a tutee or his/her folks chooses a mentor, technique for educating is totally up to the coach. Mentors can involve various apparatuses for this.

Chapter 7: Bring in Cash from Writing for a blog:

A blogger is an individual who composes blog, by which the person can get the advancement in his blogger webpage and make it conceivable to produce cash however much they need.

Writing for a blog is one of the most incredible ways of bringing in cash online without speculation. There are many contributing to a blog stages like Blogger, Word Press, Type cushion and so on, however there are some writing for a blog stages that can be utilized for publishing content to a blog and bringing in cash on the web.

A blog (an abbreviated rendition of "weblog") is a web-based diary or educational site showing data in switch sequential request, with the most recent posts showing up first, at the top. It is a stage where an essayist or a gathering of journalists share their perspectives on a singular subject.

What is the reason for a blog?

There are many motivations to begin a blog for individual use and just a modest bunch serious areas of strength for of for business contributing to a blog. Contributing to a blog for business, tasks, or whatever else that could bring you cash has an exceptionally direct reason - to rank your site higher in Google SERPs, a.k.a. increment your perceivability.

As a business, you depend on shoppers to continue to purchase your items and administrations. As another business, you depend on publishing content to a blog to assist you with getting to expected customers and catch their eye. Without contributing to a blog, your site would stay undetectable, while running a blog makes you accessible and cutthroat.

Thus, the fundamental motivation behind a blog is to interface you to the important crowd. Another is to support your traffic and send quality prompts your site.

The more continuous and better your blog entries are, the higher the opportunities for your site to get found and visited by your main interest group. This implies that a blog is a viable lead age instrument. Add an incredible source of inspiration (CTA) to your substance, and it will change over your site traffic into top notch leads. A blog likewise permits you to feature your specialty authority and construct a brand.

At the point when you utilize your specialty information for making instructive and drawing in posts, it constructs entrust with your crowd. Incredible publishing content to a blog makes your business look more dependable, which is particularly significant on the off chance that your image is as yet youthful and genuinely obscure. It guarantees presence on the web and specialty authority simultaneously.

Blog structure

The presence of sites has changed after some time, and nowadays writes incorporate a wide assortment of things and gadgets. In any case, most sites actually incorporate a few standard elements and designs.

Here are normal elements that an ordinary blog will include:

- Header with the menu or route bar.

- Primary substance region with featured or most recent blog entries.

- Sidebar with social profiles, most loved content, or source of inspiration.

- Footer with pertinent connections like a disclaimer, protection strategy, contact page, and so forth.

The above model is the fundamental design of the typical blog. Every thing has its own significance and assists guests with exploring through your blog.

Sites and sites

Many individuals actually keep thinking about whether there is any contrast between a blog and a site. What is a blog and what is a site? Separating between the two today is considerably seriously testing. Many organizations are incorporating online journals into their sites too, which further confounds the two.

What separates web journals from sites?

Web journals need incessant updates. Genuine instances of this incorporate a food blog sharing feast recipes or an organization expounding on their industry news.

Writes additionally advance peruser commitment. Perusers get an opportunity to remark and voice their various worries and considerations to the local area. Blog proprietors update their webpage with new blog entries consistently.

Turn into a Consultant

A free worker procuring compensation per work is known as a consultant. They ordinarily take up transient errands. They partake in the opportunity of telecommuting at adaptable times. Along these lines, it permits them to adjust their work-life better. For example, a specialist is a visual planner who takes up tasks to plan logos for an organization.

A consultant can work all day or parttime, contingent upon their agreement. These self employed entities start their work with a marked agreement and a foreordained expense according to the time and exertion they should place in to finish that responsibility. The installment likewise relies upon the consultant, and they can decide to get compensated in light of hour, day, or undertaking.

Instances of Specialists

A few writers function as specialists in which they select a story they wish to provide details regarding, and in the wake of forming their report, they offer it to the bidder they consider fit. Essentially, website specialists or application engineers restrict with a specific organization and individual and create their application or plan their site. After finishing of the task, they continue on toward the following client.

Make and Sell hand crafted things:

However long you have a good web association and some time to burn, setting up an internet based store is simple. Why pick this choice?

Since setting up your own store requires no speculation or unique prerequisites, you can sell anything thing you need. All you want is sufficient excitement for selling items and great showcasing abilities.

Are there any prerequisites? - You needn't bother with any accreditation to begin an internet based store. As a matter of fact, in the event that you haven't sold anything before then beginning all along will be hard for anybody in light of the fact that the market is cutthroat to the point that nobody.

Information section occupations:

Whether you're searching for a simple and speedy method for bringing in cash on the web, or a nonstop stream of pay without such a large number of actual prerequisites, information section occupations can give that.

These are the ideal arrangement on the off chance that you needn't bother with any preparation or involvement with regions, for example, deals, advertising, IT advancement, illustrations plan and different capabilities where your composing abilities might prove to be useful. There is certainly no greater method for bringing in cash from home than with some assistance from somebody you know.

Are there any prerequisites? - One more kind of work opportunity ought to have the option to utilize any PC gadget like mobile phones and tablets.

These positions are one of the most famous ways of bringing in cash online without speculation. Information passage occupations come in all shapes and sizes. However, they regularly include arranging, sorting, interpreting, or contributing information into a data set or bookkeeping sheet.

Most information section occupations offer cutthroat compensation rates and you can function so a lot or as little as you need to accommodate your timetable.

Assuming you partake in the possibility that you can decide your own schedule for these kinds of positions, then this might be the sort of occupation for you. If not, there are then again other incredible open doors accessible!

Remote helpers:

Remote helpers (VAs) is the new term for Homegrown Partners or Live-in Parental figures. It's simply a method for portraying ladies who give house keeper and family administrations through web stages like Consultant and Fiverr.

This lucrative action is filling quickly in numerous different nations all over the planet in light of minimal expense base contrasted with conventional staffing model.

Numerous sites are acquiring fame by employing VAs and they pay very well as well!

Thus, on the off chance that you have Web information enough why not.

Sell old things on OLX, Quickr or jiji:

This is a method for procuring on the off chance that you need some extra free cash. You can sell your old stuff on the web or through nearby characterized or selling sites like OLX, Quikr and jiji and so forth. You won't ever understand what individuals truly need until they come to get the thing that you are offering at an extremely modest cost.

In this cycle, keep away from the hustle of purchasing stuff that will not be sold in the future and get more cash-flow when another person gets it at the maximum by posting the things in right class on OLX and Quikr. This entire cycle can bring in insane cash.

Make recordings or Sell photographs:

This is an extremely well known work that can be made without speculation. The profit are not immense, yet enough to make a pay of around $20/hr. assuming you do it hourly.

Assuming you have great and creative abilities, this is the most effective way to bringing in cash on the web. With video or photograph altering and transferring on YouTube, Google drive and different sites it is conceivable of procuring more than $50/hr. effectively from home.

You needn't bother with any specialized abilities for this since most altering programming's out there can be utilized by fledglings despite the fact that some like Adobe Photoshop has a better quality.

Manual human test Composing Position

Before, manual human test composing position were well known on the grounds that they required no venture and required no capabilities.

Notwithstanding, the vast majority of these positions have dialed back or halted by and large. Manual human test composing position are currently tracked down for the most part on little sites that offer them as a way for clients to bring in cash while they attempt to develop their site.

These sorts of destinations are regularly not notable or solid. Subsequently, they don't pay well by the same token.

That being said, manual human tests are still around in certain spots, yet they're not normal any longer.

We suggest taking a gander at different open doors like record work, tracking down ways of selling things on the web, (for example, you own or handcrafted specialties), or taking reviews for organizations that will repay you with money or gift vouchers.

Review Filling Position

One of the most mind-blowing ways of bringing in cash online with no speculation is through study filling position. These are the sort of positions which expect you to finish up studies for various organizations. Then you get compensated for each overview that you complete.

The beneficial thing about these positions is that they offer speedy money, and you can make various installments each month.

One of the most famous review destinations is Swagbucks, which has a large number of individuals around the world. Whenever you join on Swagbucks, they'll grant you with focuses for taking overviews. You'll likewise get rewards for alluding companions to the site also!

form Filling Position

Form filling position are one of the most straightforward ways of bringing in cash online with practically no speculation by composing. The most outstanding aspect of this sort of occupation is that it tends to be done when you need.
So you'll have all the more leisure time in your day to do different things. Structure filling position are ideal for individuals who have a bustling

timetable since they don't call for much investment by any means. You should simply enter essential data into a structure and get compensated for your work!

Transcription

Transcription occupations are one method for bringing in cash with next to no speculation. These positions are exceptionally famous, and they pay well in light of the fact that translating sound or video is a tedious cycle. That is the reason many individuals who lack opportunity and willpower to translate these records recruit experts to do it for them.

ranscription occupations can be found on sites like Amazon Translate, and Scribie. The occupation might expect you to work at your own speed, which could be an alluring reward.

You could try and get compensated more assuming you work rapidly! Assuming you go after record positions online with no speculation, ensure that you know how long your sound tracks are prior to going after the position.

This will assist you with figuring out what sort of hardware you might require to finish the responsibility.

Language Interpretation

How much cash you can make each hour is really significant. Assuming that you type at a pace of 40 words each moment, that is about $14 each hour.

In the event that you're conversant in two dialects, you might actually get two times as much cash-flow by deciphering content.

For instance, assuming your composing speed is 60 words each moment, that is more than $28 each hour! That may not seem like a great deal to certain individuals, yet it truly accumulates throughout every day.

It additionally gives you additional opportunity to live life to the fullest and less time on exhausting assignments like information section.

Content Composition

You might have seen that there are numerous sites out there extending to various sorts of composing employment opportunities. A large number of these destinations post content composing position.

Content scholars are liable for making unique substance for a site or blog. In the event that you've at any point contemplated writing for a blog, this is an extraordinary method for beginning!

For these positions, you can expound on anything at all that intrigues you. It very well may be something as different as cooking, design, or cultivating.

You don't need to stress over being restricted to only one sort of subject. And that implies that anything is possible with regards to how much cash you can make utilizing this technique.

www.ingramcontent.com/pod-product-compliance
Lightning Source LLC
Chambersburg PA
CBHW050320220526
45465CB00005B/2064